Kites

Didier Carpentier
Joël Bachelet

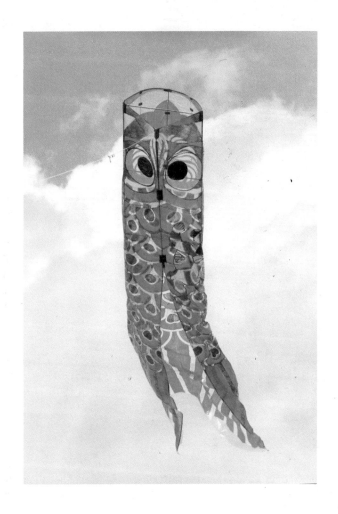

EP PUBLISHING LIMITED

The authors, in collaboration with Claudie HUANG and Emmanuella CARPENTIER, would like to acknowledge the following for their valuable assistance:

For the kites: Jean-Louis BOUISSET, President of the Kite Club of France, Nina MITZ of Japan Air Lines, Christine LINGARD and Robert PALMACCI of the International Herald Tribune, Teizo HASHIMOTO, Tsutomu HIROI, Mitsuo OKATAKE, Monique ARRADON. Chantal BARRET, Michel BERARD, André CASSAGNES, Georges CAVIN, Michel COLLARD, Robert DEVAUTOUR, Alain DIATKINE. Christian DRAN, M. FOURRE, M. OUDRY, Chris KNOWLES, Jacqueline MONNIER, Jean-Michel TOURNOUX, Claude WEISBUCH. Janette OSTIER and Laurent CHASTEL.

Design by Henri FUMAGALI, Roger GARIN. Photographs by the authors. Translated by Pierrick PICOT and Barbara TOMBS.

CONTENTS

From Past to Present

The kite probably originated in China about 4000 years ago.

Certain theories would suggest that the principle of flight could have been discovered at about the same time by several civilisations, although quite independently, but without doubt the earliest records we have come from the East.

Whichever theories are recognised as valid, the credit for the original discovery must lie with the wind. For instance, it is said that the first "kite" was inspired by seeing the wind-filled sails of fishing boats or a Chinese farmer's hat being whipped away by the wind.

Ancient China abounds in stories about kite-flying. An old textbook records that the wooden bird of Kungshu Phan remained in the air for three days. It is also said that whilst General Han Hsin was besieging a particular palace, he used the kite quite ingeniously to measure the distance of the tunnel he needed to dig in order to reach the palace walls.

In 1282, Marco Polo gave in his "Description of the World" an extremely accurate study of the principle of kite-flying, which by this time had spread through the world.

In Eastern countries, kite-flying has kept an essentially religious and mythical significance. It is used in certain celebrations to signify, for instance, Happiness, Birth, Fertility and Victory.

Kunizada, nineteenth-century print.

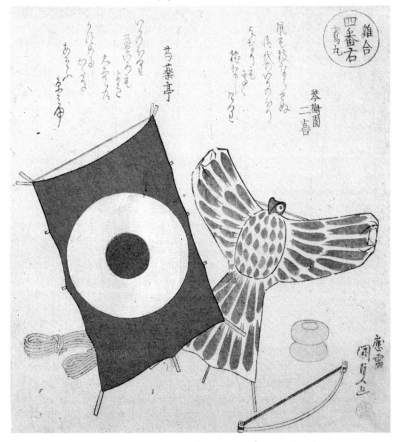

The Japanese were the first people to encourage kite-flying but, whilst the Chinese exploited its technical and functional aspects, the Japanese attached a greater religious significance to it, as shown by the many symbolical records and paintings throughout the ages (the Dragon represented Prosperity, the tortoise Long Life, while others symbolised Good Fortune, Evil Spirits, Hope, The Good Catch of Fish, Knowledge, etc.).

It is said that there was once a law forbidding kite flyers to use their kites to carry men. Yet an early example of such an attempt is shown in the following story. The famous Samurai warrior, Tumetomo, exiled on the island of Hachijo, constructed a large kite which was to bear his son across the waves to safety. It is also said that workmen used kites to carry the necessary materials for them to build towers.

The application of kite-flying was not always used for such peaceful purposes, however, as we see in the story of a reckless robber who tried to steal the golden dolphin from the Temple of Nagayo, using a man-carrying kite. The kite did not bring luck, for he was captured and thrown into boiling oil.

In Japan and Annam, the Boy's Festival is on the fifth day of the fifth month when large kites are flown to celebrate the birth of male children. On this occasion, the kites generally take the form of fish, particularly the carp, symbolic of the "Son's" progress through the river of "Life".

In Korea, it is the custom to write the name of the child and his date of birth on a paper kite. Once the kite has climbed high enough, the line is cut and the kite carried away by the wind. In this way, evil spirits are borne away and cannot torment the child.

The most famous fighting kite is without doubt the "Nagasaki Hata". Also found in Korea and China, this kite is renowned for its excellent manoeuvrability and directional control and is often equipped with a cutting device, such as ground glass glued to the line, below the bridle. The aim of the fight was to cut the opponent's line. The "Nagasaki Hata" differs from its Indian counterpart in the absence of the support fin at the tail.

The kite, so well known in the West today, was already used in Malaysia, Indonesia and on the island of Java, many centuries ago. At that time it had the classic trapezoidal shape which was flown flat or bowed – and it was this very type of kite that William A. Eddy, a journalist from New Jersey, introduced in America in 1890.

Although much disputed, Europe has traditionally suggested that the kite was invented by the Greek General Archytas of Tarentum (430 – 360 B.C.) who was both a soldier and a statesman. It is said that he was able to build a wooden replica of a dove, which flew successfully without falling to the ground. But it is also thought that the construction of his dove may have been inspired by Chinese bird kites.

Throughout the Middle-Ages, there were many variations of kite-flying. In 1589, Giambattista della Porta gave a description of a kite which apparently looked like the traditional Chinese form. He also suggested uses for the kite, such as lifting fireworks, lanterns, etc. The lozenge kite form appeared in Holland as early as 1618, in an engraving of Middleburg. This gives further support to the idea that the Dutch merchants played an important role in introducing the kite to the West.

By the beginning of the eighteenth century, kite-flying had become a very popular pastime throughout Europe. It was also developed for scientific research, although it was not until 1749 that the first experiment was recorded – that of Alexander Wilson's experiment in Scotland. He measured the variations of temperature at different altitudes by fastening thermometers to half a dozen kites tied to a single flying line, 915 metres long. This technique, called "flying in train", is used to fly several kites at the same time. This experiment provides us with the first written account of the "flying in train" technique being used.

Hokuba, eighteenth-century print.

In 1752, Benjamin Franklin carried out a number of experiments on lightning by using a kite. Between 1799 and 1809, George Cayley studied the basic principles of aeronautics through kite-flying and discovered the principles of the lifting properties of the air. In 1830, George Pocock was able to lift his daughter Martha 90 metres into the air. She had been tied into an armchair which was suspended from a kite, and thus one of the first recognised man-lifting attempts was achieved. He also designed a char-volant: a carriage, pulled by a kite, which travelled 200 kilometres through the English countryside in one day.

Last century, kite-flying found various applications. Different models were studied and tested, more or less successfully. Most of them were inspired by the old dream which man was soon to turn into reality – that of flying.

In 1894, J. Woodbridge Davis used Colladon's technique to equip a dirigible kite which could be used to rescue people stranded on shipwrecked boats.

In 1887, E. D. Archibald took the first aerial photograph with a camera fastened to the flying line. All sorts of other devices (mainly meteorological) were also fastened to kites. W. R. Birt experimented with a flat hexagonal kite, stabilised by two lateral lines, and controlled from the ground by the operator using two flying lines.

The properties of the dihedral kite were later discovered by William A. Eddy. They were used for a while at the Blue Hill Observatory, but shortly after were replaced by Lawrence Hargrave's box kite. Another great name which should be mentioned in connection with man-lifting kites is B.F.S. Baden-Powell, the brother of the founder of the Scout Movement. He refused to acknowledge the advantages of the principles developed by Hargrave, and 1894 saw his own successful ascent 3 metres high in a nacelle suspended from a hexagonal kite with a span of 11 metres. He realised the danger of such an operation and, the following year, developed the Levitor, a system of flying in train using between four and seven hexagonal kites.

On 12 December 1901, Marconi established radio contact between Cornwall and Newfoundland, the aerial being raised using approximately 120 metres Baden-Powell's Levitor kite.

Until now, human ascents had been made by suspending the person to be lifted from the actual kite line, but the American Charles J. Lawson managed to fly within the structure of his biplane kite, similar to the aeroplane. Meanwhile, in Germany, Otto Lilienthal was constructing his first gliders.

In America, Samuel Franklin Cody became a well-known character in the history of kite-flying. He improved the man-lifting system by devising a model which he demonstrated in 1901 to the War Office.

Harunobu, eighteenth-century print.

The model was made up of a nacelle for the passenger which was attached to a line of kites. In the case of war, the nacelle could be fitted with a telescope, telephone, camera and even firearms.

In 1903, Cody crossed the English Channel in a boat drawn by a similar model.

Around 1913, many clubs and organisations had been created and a large international competition was held at Spa in Belgium.

Then followed the First World War and kites were used as a means of observation. But they were soon replaced by balloons and aeroplanes; such inventions were quickly scooped up from their inventors and used for industrial research and manufacturing.

Rapidly the development of these techniques brought about further progress. Even so, the principle of the "flying in train" technique was used by the Germans during the Second World War to make observations at sea from submarines.

It is at this point that the ways of the kite and the aeroplane divide. Now that man's time-old dream had turned into reality, kite-flying became a game once again, but despite all that had been achieved, the dream of flying freely without mechanical constraint remained one of man's greatest aspirations. Such aspirations have been fulfilled once again with the reappearance, under its contemporary form, of the bird-man, the hang-glider, "free flight".

Meanwhile, Alexander Graham Bell, the inventor of the telephone, was experimenting with a new type of kite with tetrahedral cellular structures. He built a wide range of models, the biggest being made of 3393 cells.

In 1948, Francis Rogallo perfected the famous delta wing kites, and the subsequent related models, bringing even greater improvements to them.

After 1950, new models appeared without a frame, made from flexible pockets which fill with air when in flight. Despite their numerous advantages, they have not succeeded in ousting the traditional models which are still found in Japan, where the largest kites in the world (Hoshubana) are constructed.

Necessary Precautions

Avoid flying kites in stormy weather.

The harmless character of the kite makes it a safe object, suitable for everyone. Nevertheless, elementary precautions should be taken.

The proximity of high tension electric cables, for example, can be a real danger, and we cannot advise kite flyers too strongly to keep a good distance from them. If the kite suddenly drops onto the cables, you could receive a fatal electric shock through the flying line.

It should be remembered that these risks are increased in damp conditions and also that it is unwise to fly a kite in stormy weather. Although such a famous character as Franklin obtained satisfactory results in the course of his experiments on electricity in the air, we would advise the beginner against trying out this sort of thing.

In order to avoid careless accidents, the kite-flyer should keep away from airports and roads, and preferably choose open land. Indeed, it is best to avoid areas where there are trees and buildings.

Some precautions must also be observed in the use of the reel and the handling of the flying line. We would suggest that the kite flyer uses special gloves to protect his hands against unpleasant burns and cuts which can be caused by the flying line.

Give other kite-flyers sufficient room, so that the lines of your kites do not tangle, causing them to fall.

Be careful not to create havoc in the poultry farm! Amusing as this may sound, it is meant in all seriousness, for there is an old story that poultry are born with the gift of being able to detect their natural enemies (birds of prey) and greet their approach with general commotion. Our peaceful feathered friends have a rather limited sense of perception, and are likely to confuse kites with birds of prey once they see one of these huge paper birds appear in the sky, motionless and mysterious, apparently ready to pounce at any moment on its victim.

But don't let us allow sensitivity and imagination to carry us away. The story of Mr. Cavin could have lost all sense of proportion and become an unprecedented mistake in the history of our noble "bird". One beautiful summer's evening, he was flying one of his latest creations, oval in shape and made out of polystyrene.

This splendid kite soared 1500 metres into the air and, in the higher spheres of the atmosphere, soon came into contact with an air current moving in the opposite direction. This strange object shining in the sunset did not remain unnoticed by the local population, who watched the proceedings in amazement.

On several occasions the object would move slightly and then stop. The police, who had been alerted at once, started to investigate, but it wasn't until the U.F.O. slowly descended that they were finally able to identify it.

Description of the kite

The kite is an aircraft belonging to the family of the aerodynes, that is to say, devices which are heavier-than-air, as opposed to aerostats (balloons, montgolfiers, dirigibles, etc.) which are lighter than air. Its main characteristic lies in the fact that it is tethered to the ground by a line. It is maintained in the air without any engine but simply by the force of the wind. The kite is made up of 5 components:

— the reel (or *winch* for large kites)
— the flying-line
— the bridle
— the framework
— the cover

Each of these components has a specific role and function.

The Reel

This is used to wind or unwind the line and to store it on the ground.

The flying-line

The line serves as the means of communication between the kite and the handler. It is through the line that the handler becomes aware of the various thrust forces to which the kite is subjected. The break strength coefficient which prevents the severing of the line is around 6. This means that a kite "pulling" 3 kg, must be fastened to a line with a resistance of 6 x 3 kg.

The bridle

The bridle is made of at least two legs, and its role consists of distributing the forces of drag proportionately throughout the kite. For this reason, the tying points on the framework must be carefully chosen. The relationship between the lengths of the legs of the bridle is also very important and should be carefully calculated. The legs must meet at one point called the towing point, the only exception to this being the dirigible kites.

The Framework

The framework forms the skeleton of the kite, on which the cover will be stretched. It is made from longerons (running lengthwise) and spars (running widthwise). The framework can be made from metal or plastic, or from bamboo, reed or balsa, according to the type of kite.

The Cover

The cover includes all the "membranes" of the kite. They can be flexible or stretched taut between the various sections of the framework.

Amongst the other parts making up the kite, we should also mention:

1 — the bracing strings, which in certain cases connect the main points of the frame (their role is essentially to make it rigid);

2 — the tail whose role is to stabilise the kite.

The elements of the frame of cellular kites are on different planes.

1. Leading edge – 2. Forward cell – 3. Forward bridle point – 4. Wing – 5. Forward spar – 6. Vent – 7. Forward leg of bridle – 8. Towing ring – 9. Rear leg of bridle – 10. Rear spar – 11. Lower longeron – 12. Trailing edge – 13. Rear bridle point – 14. Longeron – 15. Rear cell.

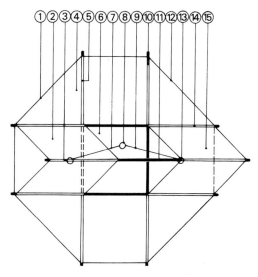

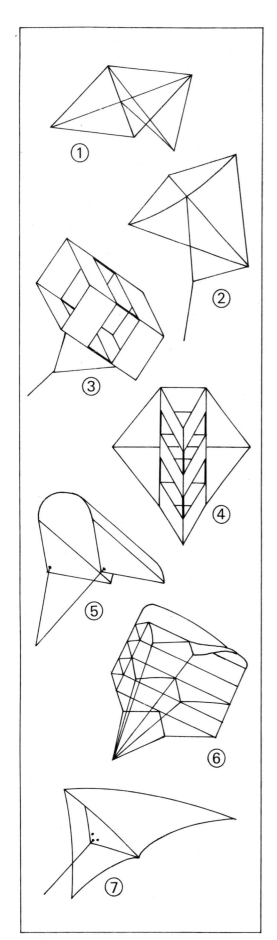

Classification of kites

Kites can be classified into various groups. They used to be grouped according to their covers (rigid kites or flexible kites) or the number of plances (monoplane kites, simple kites, dihedral or bowed kites, cellular kites). Today they fall into eight main types: flat or plane-surface kites, dihedral or bowed kites, cellular kites, sleds, parafoils, parachutes, parawings, and dirigibles.

Flat Kites

These are certainly the oldest known kites. At their most attractive, they can challenge a good number of their successors; the Chinese centipede, for example, is nothing more than a succession of small flat circles, placed one after the other. The Thailand serpent is also based on the same system of the flat kites. The main characteristic of this type of kite is that the surface of the cover is flat. The elements of the framework are all situated on the same plane. Tails can be added, depending on their stability.

Flat kites can have different shapes ranging from the simplest to the most complicated form of square, circle, lozenge, regular hexagonal, irregular hexagonal, etc.

Dihedral or bowed kites

There have been many variations on this basic style for centuries. It was only during the nineteenth century, however, that the reasons for their good stability were discovered. Most of the fighting kites can be included in this group. The main feature of these kites lies in their cover which is lightly folded in two or bowed (in both cases) according to the axis of symmetry.

Cellular Kites

Cellular kites can be divided into two groups, flexible kites and box kites. Their resemblance comes from the fact that the elements of their framework are positioned on different planes, as opposed to the flat kites which are on a single plane. Whereas the elements of the frame of the flexible cellular kites are not interconnected between planes, those of the box kites are, resulting in a much more solid structure.

Sleds

Sleds are very flexible. The longerons of the framework are not linked by spars but are completely independent. Thus they can be rolled lengthwise and easily stored without having to be dismantled entirely. The sleds generally have two lateral legs for the bridle. Rather unusually, they have not been modified throughout the years and only four models exist. It should also be mentioned that their angle of flight is situated exceptionally at 60°.

Parawings

Parawings, the forerunner of the delta kite, were designed by Francis Rogallo. The cover has a centre crease, usually along a

1. Flat – 2. Dihedral – 3. Box – 4. Flexible cellular – 5. Sled – 6. Parafoil – 7. Delta.

longitudinal axis (the diagonal axis for square covers and the symmetrical elevation for covers shaped like an isosceles triangle). This group also includes the delta kite where the longerons are made rigid by a cross-bar.

Parafoils

Parafoils are frameless and made of a series of airfoil cells, sewn side by side in a row. The forward end of these cells is open to the wind. The number of cells varies from four to thirteen according to the model. Parafoils are also characterised by three small triangular keels underneath each section. The legs of the bridle are attached to the tip of the keels.

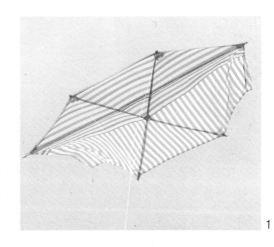

Parachutes

This type of kite is a variation of the parachute itself. Needless to say, it has no frame and the cover is made of several strips of fabric sewn together by segments. The legs are fastened to the outer edge of the cover.

Dirigible Kites

These are characterised by two separate flying lines which the handler can manipulate with both hands, either from two separate reels or by means of a cross-bar, where the flying lines are fastened to each end.

The best examples of this group are the flexifoils which are a recent innovation. These are made from sections of small pockets sewn together and fastened to the flying line at both ends by a small rigid stick.

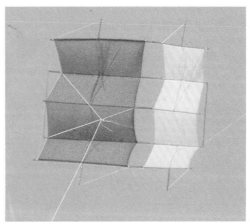

There are other types of kites (e.g. the W-Form kite), which by the very nature of their structures belong to the box kite family although they do not have proper cells. Polystyrene kites also belong to a group related to the box kite. They are characterised by the material itself which allows the kite flyer the maximum of originality in his search for a shape.

The origins of the gliding kites lie with model planes. They are devices which are based on the principles of the dihedral kites – as are aeroplanes.

1. Irregular hexagonal kite belonging to flat kite category – 2. W Form kite – 3. Parafoil – 4. Flexifoil.

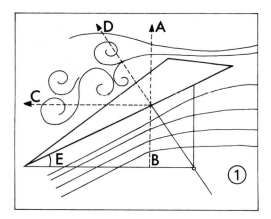

1. Diagram showing the forces acting upon a kite – 2. Incorrect horizontal position (cannot catch the wind) – 3. Ideal position for strong winds – 4. Ideal position for light winds – 5. Incorrect position (the kite blocks the wind).

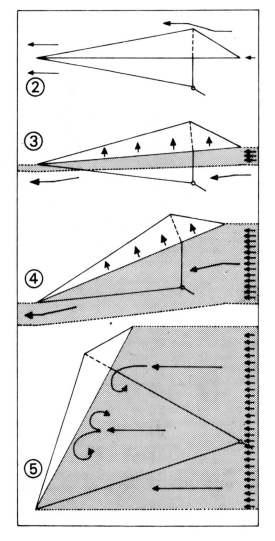

Physical aspects

Although the amateur gets much more pleasure from making his own kite, he can never be sure of getting the same satisfaction from flying it unless he has respected the basic principles of aerodynamics. It may well be that a very attractive kite does not possess the qualities necessary for it to fly, i.e. lightness, resistance, stability.

To avoid this, follow the advice given below, for the configuration of the kite is of prime importance if it is to fly well.

Density

Whilst the kite is being built, you must try to find out the best possible ratio between resistance and lightness, keeping in mind that kites are heavier-than-air devices. For this purpose we can use a very simple formula from physics:

$$d = \frac{W}{S}$$

d being the density of the kite (or weight by unit of surface), W its weight, and S its cover area. The weight of the kite includes framework, cover and bridle.

The ratio must be around 1 kilogram per square metre for strong winds. For moderate winds, the ratio is 0.5 kg/m² and for light winds 0.2 kg/m². For example, a kite weighing 200 g and covering a surface of 1m² will have a ratio of 0.2.

It is important that beginners keep within these limits.

The Angle of flight

The position of the kite in flight is important. It is dependent upon the relationship between three forces – lift, gravity and drag. These forces are said to be concentrated upon the centre of lift (A), the centre of gravity (B) and the centre of drag (C). These forces when combined form the centre of pressure (D).

The bridle should be adjusted to the axis of the centre of pressure.

The best position for the angle of attack (E) is generally between 30° and 35° according to the speed. It is the only position which enables the wind to exert lift on the under surface of the kite.

If the kite is structurally well-balanced and correctly fastened to the flying line, you should not encounter any problem and the kite should climb steadily.

A high angle should be chosen for slow speeds and a low angle for higher speeds, taking into account that turbulence, caused by air breaking on the upper face of the kite, will slow down its ascent. Indeed, although between a 30° and 35° angle, the wind pressure will lift the kite, turbulence has the contrary effect.

Stability

Maximum lift can be achieved when the kite is flying into the wind. For this, good directional and lateral stability is required.

Generally speaking, the stability of the kite is dependent upon its proportions being correct and the weights and planes being correctly balanced from the axis of symmetry, as well as the lengths of the legs being equal. As you can see, the design of the kite must observe the rules of symmetry and its measurements must be determined with great precision. The rule applies to all types of kites without exception, and the kite's stability is dependent upon it being strictly observed.

The cover of dihedral kites is characterised by two inclined planes crossing on the axis of symmetry. This results in a better distribution of the airflow on the lower face of the dihedral kite than on the cover of the flat kites. The dihedral angle automatically restores the equilibrium which may have been affected by a gust of wind. In case of disequilibrium, the wing A B (fig. 6) presents a greater area to the air flow than does the wing B C. Pressure is thus greater on wing A B.

There are other methods of providing a kite with stability, the most basic being the tail which is essential for flat kites. It is also possible to brace certain elements of the framework, as, for example, in the case of the Eddy kite.

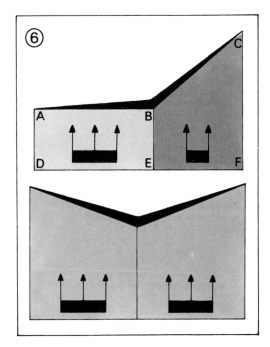

The dihedral kite automatically restores equilibrium.

Relationship between the stabilizing forces ➡
and lifting forces. ---➤

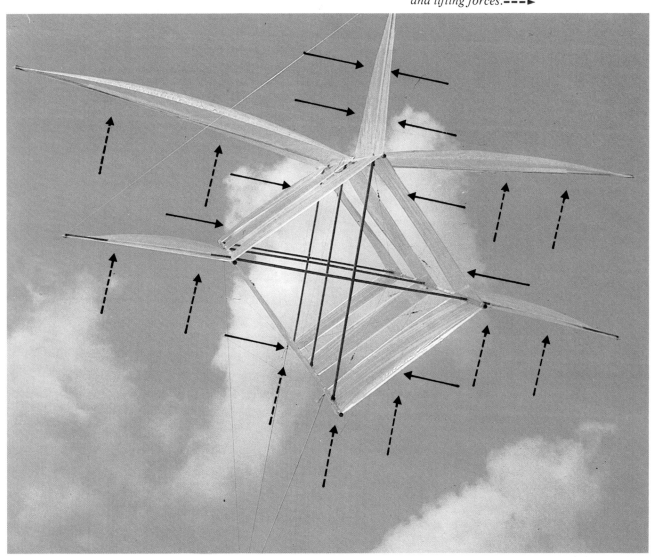

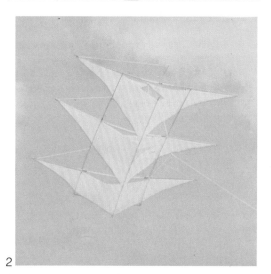

Categories

Being aware of the density and type of the kite is not enough to know whether the kite can fly in a strong or light wind. It is thus important to establish the limits within which flying is possible, and to be able to appreciate the wind speed at the time of the take-off. Indeed, not all kites fly under the same conditions.

A light and flexible kite is well suited to flying in a light wind. In a strong wind, the same kite will be unable to take off and it is very likely to become twisted and torn into pieces.

A large heavy kite, built from sturdy materials, carefully designed, and able to support strong wind pressure without losing its shape, will fly admirably in bad weather, demonstrating its excellent qualities of flight. In light wind, this same kite will remain obstinately on the ground, indicating that it really is heavier than air.

Kites are divided into 3 categories: kites for light winds (force 1 and 2), for moderate winds (force 3, 4, 5), and for strong winds (force 6, 7, 8). It has been noticed that a force 2 wind exerts a pressure of 2.17 kg/m² at speeds varying from 6 to 11 km/h, a force 4 wind exerts a pressure of 6.04 kg/m² at speeds varying from 20 to 28 km/h, and a force 6 wind exerts a pressure of 10.97 kg/m² at speeds varying from 39 to 42 km/h.

Generally, it is thought that the required density for flights in light wind (below 5 metres/second) is around 0.2. The advised density for moderate to strong wind is 0.5, and a density of 1 is required for kites designed for strong winds.

Thus the density of kites is closely linked to the force of the wind, which is why it is necessary to make models which are of suitable resistance and lightness.

The flat kites, which are generally light, are very good flyers in light winds, whereas the bowed kites fly better in moderate winds and cellular kites in strong winds.

1. Kite suitable for light wind.
2. Kite suitable for moderate wind.
3. Kite suitable for strong wind.

Conditions for flight

Knowledge of the density of the kite and the speed of the wind in which it can be flown, does not enable the kite flyer to fly his kite anywhere. He must also choose a suitable launching area. For this purpose, a certain number of important factors should be taken into consideration when flying the kite – especially the lie of the land, which plays a vital role in the liveliness of ground winds.

We have already seen that the air is remarkably turbulent above uneven land, even in light wind. Trees and buildings as well as uneven terrain can also cause turbulence, and it is not until the kite is above a height of 45 metres that it will settle down.

The ideal place to launch one's kite is a perfectly flat and open piece of land, such as moorland, a beach, the shores of a lake, etc.

By the sea, winds are often steady and very stable. Their force increases gradually and evenly as the kite gains altitude. Often, variations between land and sea temperatures can completely alter the direction of the wind. Such a turn-round of 180° can present problems to even the most experienced kite-flyer, who deserves all credit if he is able to cope with such a situation successfully.

If there is no ideal location available, the kite-flyer may have to enlist the help of a second person. Indeed, turbulence can extend – even in a light breeze – to twice the height of the obstacle. Kites are very often drawn towards the cause of the turbulence. Thus, rather than flying the kite from the top of the hill, it is better to launch it from the bottom of the hill in the direction of the wind.

Winds

Winds have many characteristics: speed, direction, turbulence, direction of airstreams, etc. Ground winds can differ from winds at higher altitudes. For this reason, you should observe carefully the character and nature of the wind before flying your kite.

Differences in atmospheric temperature result in important differences in pressure which cause natural imbalances and form winds.

Winds fall into three main groups:
— local and regional persistent winds
— global persistent winds
— episodic or seasonal winds such as tornadoes, hurricanes, cyclones, anticyclones.

The winds belonging to the first group are those most suitable for kite-flying. Such winds are not caused by geophysical factors, are not too strong, and are relatively shallow.

These winds are affected only by variations in temperature between land and water, and by the geographical influence of mountains and valleys.

The strongest variations appear between the polar regions and the equator, at the time of the spring equinox, resulting in the famous March winds so popular with kite-flyers.

This period of the year was regarded as the kite-flying season, but today more and more enthusiasts can be seen flying their kites throughout the year. Could it be that today's kites are of a better quality than those of yesterday? Or perhaps the number of enthusiasts has increased?

It is extremely important in kite-flying to know the speed of the wind. This can be measured by using a very simple device such as an anemometer. In the absence of an anemometer, the kite-flyer can use the indications described in the Beaufort scale (named after the English admiral who devised it in 1806 for the captains of sailing ships). It was initially used to evaluate, with considerable accuracy, the speed of the wind at sea. Since then, it has been somewhat modified for use on the ground generally and for

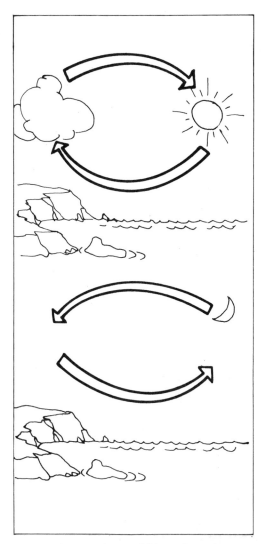

Along the sea, the wind blows from the sea to land during the day, and from the land to sea at night.

Clouds usually indicate moderate to strong winds.

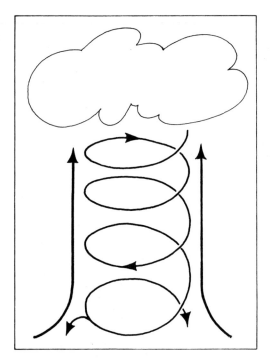

Cumulus clouds can cause thermal winds. The air under the clouds is cooler than the surrounding air, as it is shaded from the sun. This column of cooler air spirals down, disturbing the air below. Thus a warm rising air-stream can be formed at the edge of this cold front.

kite-flyers in particular, taking into account that the really keen kite-flyer will attempt to fly his kite on days when trees are uprooted by the wind. . . . During a warm spell, "thermal winds" are often observed – in fact, initially these are rising currents of warm air which occur when cool morning temperatures are followed by a sunny day. Thermal winds are formed most often above grassland or meadows. They gain speed as they rise. For this reason, kites must reach sufficient altitude before being able to rise quickly, which nevertheless may present some serious difficulties.

Kites such as rollers or dihedrals can ride the thermal winds without problem, if their line is held firmly and steadily instead of pulled jerkily.

Care should be taken, however, since the slightest breeze can blow the thermal wind away, thus abandoning the kite without support, which may result in a sudden fall. If this happens, the kite-flyer has no time to wind in the line before the kite plunges into a nosedive at high speed.

The kite may also develop excessive pull on the line, and when this happens it becomes very difficult to retrieve. The kite-flyer should release the tension of the reel slightly and walk towards his kite while winding in his line. The operation should be repeated until the kite is back in a suitable air stream.

In case this proves ineffective, a second solution may be considered, which would require the help of a second person. While the first holds the reel, the second puts a piece of strong material or a glove over the line and starts running towards the kite, sliding the cloth or glove along the line. Thus, while the line is lowered automatically, the helper holds it and the kite-flyer is able to wind in the line.

This operation should be repeated until the kite has reached a lower altitude.

The take-off

The worst technique for launching a kite is by running with it, for this is totally inefficient!

In a normal wind the kite can be launched without the slightest problem. Even after the first few metres, the kite should be able to fly by itself, without anyone holding it. But in a light wind, the kite-flyer will have to persevere if he wants to see his kite in the air. If the wind is not strong enough, then a "high-start launch" will be needed.

A high-start launch requires the help of a second person. The handler holds the line while the helper takes the kite and positions himself about 45 metres downwind of the handler. The tail of the kite should be laid on the ground so that it can stabilise the kite as soon as it rises. The handler then unwinds the line, placing it in front of him on the ground. Control is essential when launching the kite. The handler indicates to the helper when he is ready for the kite to be released, and then takes in the line as quickly as he can, hand over hand. He should try to keep the kite high. When the line shows slack, he should pull on the line slightly to regain the control of the kite. The kite should rise steadily until it reaches livelier air, when it may pull slightly on the flying line. When it has reached a certain height, the kite will maintain its ideal position, if the condition of maximum lift minimum drag has been fulfilled. It should then require more flying line and will take up the line which was neatly unwound on the ground for the launching. From now on, the kite should be flying directly from the reel.

It is possible that the kite may not rise steadily and above a certain height dips towards the horizon. The handler should give as much line as is necessary for the kite to fall, in order to attempt a second high-start launch before the kite touches the ground. The flying line should again be taken in until the kite catches the wind.

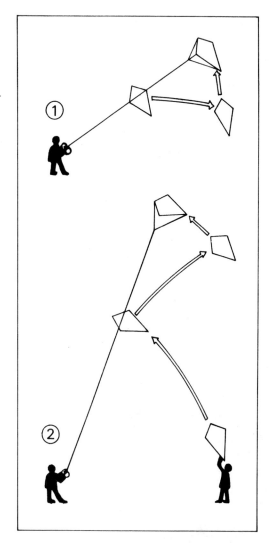

Take-off. 1: normal. 2: high-start. Photo below: position for take-off.

17

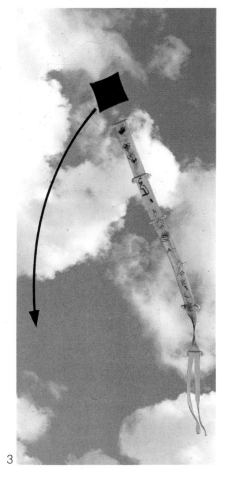

1

2

3

FAULTS	CAUSES	REMEDIES
Up and down snaking motion of the kite. 1	Lack of lateral stability.	Readjust legs on the bridle, lengthening them if necessary. Check that tension and length are equal. Add a keel if necessary.
The kite flies in large circles. 2	Unsuitable tail.	Change the material of the tail for greater flexibility. Lengthen it (it should hang like a pendulum). Tighten the rear legs without changing the angle of the bridle ring.
The kite dives to one side. 3	Unbalanced kite.	Add more weight to one side of the kite or readjust the legs of the bridle.
The kite is unsteady in flight.	The bridle is certainly too short. Too much wind.	Lengthen the legs to enable greater control and an easier ascent. Lengthen the tail.
The kite flies with too small an angle.	The bridle is too short.	Lower it progressively. Test fly the kite to check control and readjust if necessary.
The kite climbs with difficulty.	The kite is probably too heavy. A lot of drag.	Shorten the length of the tail. Wait for a stronger wind and loosen the cover more to increase its lifting surface.
The kite plunges into a nose dive and obeys commands erratically.	The bridle is too long and its towing point too low.	Close the angle of attack and release the tension of the bow. Increase the weight and length of the tail. Study again the proportions of the kite.
The kite loops quickly.	The kite is not suited to the wind and lacks stability.	Increase the bow of the cover by bracing it. Check the legs and lengthen the tail.

18

Measurement of the altitude of flight

Measuring the altitude of flight of a kite requires a few basic notions of geometry. Several methods exist based on the properties of right-angled and isosceles triangles.

The altitude should preferably be measured on the level. Otherwise, the difference in the level between the observer and the helper, who is positioned directly underneath the kite, should be taken into account. In this case, a long measuring stick should be used.

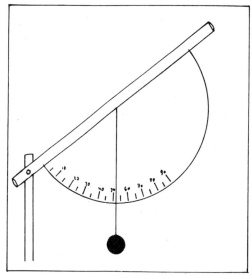

To measure the altitude of a kite in flight, a small theodolite can be made simply by attaching a plumb-line to a protractor (a theodolite is an instrument used for measuring angles on the horizon).

1   Using the 45° method

Although not absolutely accurate, the 45° method gives a good estimation of the height of the kite in flight. You will need to make a small 45° sighting protractor which is fixed to the end of the stick. The length of the stick depends upon the observer's height, i.e. the distance from ground to eye level. The stick is used to enable the measurement to be taken steadily. The protractor can be made out of thin cardboard simply by cutting a square in half diagonally. Make a hole in the right angle of the protractor and nail it to the stick. The protractor must be able to swing from the nail so that the base always returns to the horizontal, whatever the position of the stick.

You will now need two helpers. The first helper holds the flying line while the second one stands directly under the kite. The reading should be taken on the same line as that of the two helpers by holding the protractor at eye level and moving back until the kite lies on the 45° line (measured from ground level). The height is equal to the distance between the observer and the second helper.

2   Using the flying line

With this method it is necessary to know the length L of the flying line and the size of the angle A formed at the meeting point of the ground with an imaginary line going directly from the kite to the observer. The height is obtained by using the following simple formula: h = L sin A. In this formula, the distance between the observer and the helper on the one hand, and the length of the flying line on the other, are considered as similar, which means that the calculation is slightly incorrect. Indeed, by its very weight and by the effect of the wind, the flying line is slightly curved rather than completely straight. Consequently, the correct height of the kite will be slightly lower than the result obtained.

3   By sighting

Kite-flyers use this method if they wish to obtain a more accurate result. The flying line is not used in the application of the following formula.

The angle between the kite and a given point on the ground is measured, Angle A. Still on the same horizontal plane, a second measurement is taken, Angle B. Then the distance AB is measured.

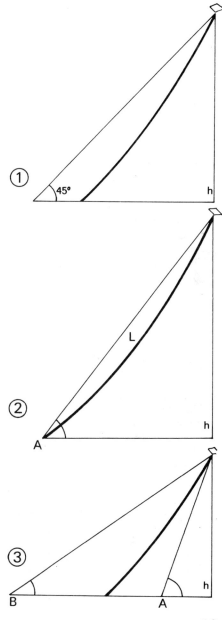

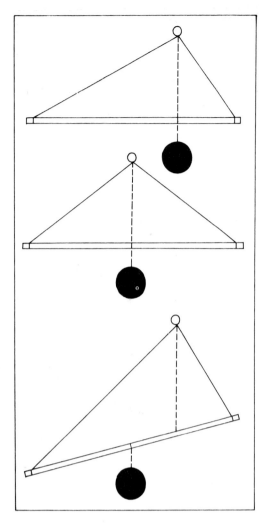

The height of the kite is calculated from these three readings by applying the following formula:

$$h = \frac{\text{Tan B} \times \text{AB} \times \text{Tan A}}{\text{Tan A} - \text{Tan B}}$$

Bridles and keels

The bridle is an extremely important part of the kite. It is made of legs which attach the kite to the flying line. They are fixed to the cover and meet at the towing point – certainly the most critical point in the geometry of a kite. If the bridle is wrongly positioned, even the most well-designed kite will not get off the ground.

All kites, with the exception of Hargrave's box kite, have bridles. The number of legs varies from one model to the next. There is no rule as to the number of legs a bridle needs. Usually the bridling technique is dependent upon the structure and the type of the kite. The multiple bridle can have between two and a hundred legs according to the kite. The role of the bridle is not only to maintain the kite in its ideal position, but also to evenly distribute the stress throughout the structure of the kite. It enables the kite to retain its original shape and avoids distortion in strong winds.

It is therefore important to establish the correct length for the legs and to find out the exact towing point where the bridle ring is to be positioned. The legs determine the angle of attack of the kite and also its position in flight in relation to the horizontal level; it is therefore essential to balance the kite.

Balancing the bridle at the centre of pressure.

The method of balancing the kite is simple. Suspend the kite by the bridle and adjust the length of the legs, so that the kite becomes perfectly level. The two-legged bridle is fixed to the central longeron and to the bridle ring. The kite should be balanced by holding the kite by the bridle ring and lifting it so that the tail end of the kite is at an angle of 20° to 30° from the horizontal level. When the legs are balanced, the kite-flyer should fasten them to the towing-ring. The towing point should be situated at about one third of the way down between the two tying points and away from the frame, at a distance equal to half of this length.

With the correct angle of the bridle, the kite has every possibility of a good take-off. Adjustments before the flight are then minimal. Nevertheless, some are necessary to adapt the kite to the weather conditions. With a high angle of attack, the area exposed to the wind is larger and more wind is deflected over the lower face of the kite; this is the basic principle which is used to adjust the bridle. When launching, the angle of attack should be higher than during flight to help the kite to catch the wind.

In strong wind, if the angle is too high the pressure of the air over the lower face of the kite may be strong enough to break the spars and tear the cover.

The centre of drag is where all the legs are joined togeher at the bridle ring. It is called the towing point. Each bridle can have one or two legs.

Another bridling system is the keel bridle which is very satisfactory as far as stability is concerned.

The two legs of the bridle are replaced by a central triangle made of material, attached underneath the cover along the longeron. The two outer sides of the triangle must have the same proportions as the bridle which has been replaced.

In order to enable the kite to be adjusted to the various winds, it is best to have two or three towing rings at the tip of the triangle. Apart from giving good lateral stability, a well-proportioned keel offers the same properties as a bridle. It exerts a downward pressure and distributes the tension evenly along the entire length of the cover, giving it uniformity and the characteristics of the dihedral kite. It helps to ensure a smooth flight and facilitates control.

Light wind kites are often built with a rudder at the tail end. As we saw for the keels, the rudder should be correctly proportioned and it should not be too small to be effective.

Most of the keels and rudders take advantage of the downward pressure exerted by the flying line.

The spring-loaded bridles are especially designed to cancel the effects of unwanted pressure, correcting the angle of attack whilst the kite is in flight.

The bridles of the dirigible kites belong to a different category. A good number of kites are equipped with them, and they are fixed on double, and even quadruple, flying lines. The handling of these lines is simple: the kite-flyer holds one or two in each hand, and he can make his kite turn, dive or rise in the sky.

Keel and rudder of a roller.

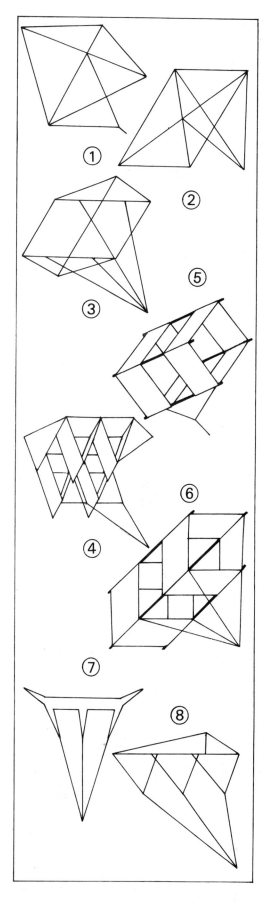

1. Two-legged bridle – 2. Three-legged bridle – 3. Four-legged bridle – 4. Compound bridle – 5. Bridle for box kite flown on one edge – 6. Bridle for box kite flown flat – 7 and 8. Multiple bridle.

Knots

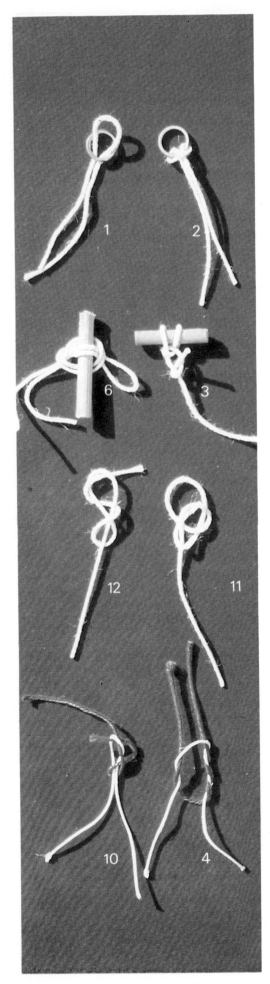

1 & 2. The "lark's head" is used to secure the legs to the towing ring. It can also be used to attach secondary lines to the main line – for example, flying-in-train.

3. This round turn and two half hitches is excellent for tethering a flying line (always attach to a smooth surface).

4. The "surgeon's knot" is a reliable and secure knot, used mainly in the making of kite frames.

5. The "fisherman's knot" should be chosen when joining two lengths of natural fibre of equal or varying diameter.

6. The "toggle hitch" gives easy curves which are less likely to break. It is ideal for attaching secondary lines.

7. This knot, the "blood knot", is used particularly for joining both nylon and monofilament lines. Its main application is in kite making.

8. Here is a knot – the "double sheet bend" – which is ideal for joining two lines of different materials and thickness. The joins should be tested.

9. The traditional method for stowing a multiple bridle to avoid tangles. Just pull the towing loops to untie it.

10. The "tiller hitch" is well suited for attaching a secondary line to a toggle hitch. It is a very secure knot which can also be untied quickly.

11. This knot, the "bowline", is especially adapted for joining two lines which may be subject to a slight pull. It is used above all in the construction of the frame.

12. The "half blood" knot is generally used to join synthetic and monofilament lines of equal diameter.

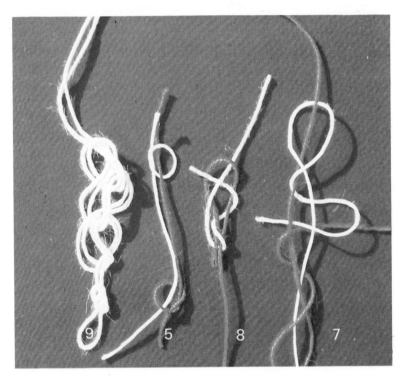

Tails

Tails and wind-socks provide directional stability. Their main function is to create drag which can be reduced or increased as necessary. It is important to distinguish between the effects caused by their weight and those caused by the drag.

In a strong wind, pressures exerted on the lower face of the kite can be compensated for by the stabilising action of the tail. Thus, the length of the tail should be adapted to the velocity of the wind. As a rule, tails are about 7 times longer than the frame of their kites.

Before flying your kite properly, it is a good idea to have a few trial attempts using tails of various lengths. They should be neither too long nor too short. They should fly gracefully in the air, counterbalancing the movement of the kite without any backlash.

Whilst not all large kites need tails, flat kites cannot fly without them. As winds are not always steady, it is very likely that their speed will increase at the very moment when the kite is climbing. In this case, if the kite is to climb well, the tail would need to be flexible and able to lengthen or retract as necessary. This is the principle of a wind-sock, which is no more than a cylindrical piece of cloth through which the wind blows. It is usually open at both ends, and automatically regulates the airflow by adapting itself to the velocity of the wind. If it drops too much, its angle of flight can be corrected simply by pulling on the line.

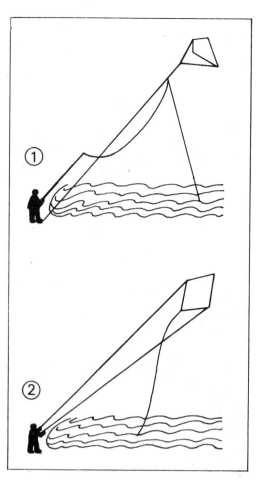

1. Fishing with a rod – 2. Fishing-line attached to flying line of dirigible kite.

Wind-sock.

Applications of kite-flying

The history of kite-flying has shown us how imaginative and astute our ancestors were. There has been a constant flow of ideas, ranging from the first Chinese bird to the delta kite, not forgetting the man-lifting kite. The origin of the aeroplane, and indeed many more inventions, is owed to the kite. In addition to this, numerous other applications have been found. It is used for scientific research, in particular in atmospheric or meteorological research, in radio transmissions and for aerial photography. In the field of navigation, it is used for rescue and for towing. It is also employed for military purposes in signalling and observation. It can also be used for advertising by attaching slogans to it.

In spite of its many practical applications, kite-flying remains a genuine hobby and a sport which is extremely popular.

Camera attached to flying line.

Winding reels

Winding reels can take various forms. The size of the reel is determined by the size of the kite, and the length of the flying line.

A good reel is one which can be easily handled. The role it plays in a successful take-off is often underestimated. However, quick control of the flying line, a steady take-off, and resistance to thrusts, all depend on the reel.

The type of take-off will determine the type of reel to be used. There are three types of reel: bobbins, simple stick winders and plyboard winders.

With bobbins, the line is wound around a central core.

With stick winders (a piece of wood, a can or a tin), the line is simply wound around it.

Plyboard winders are certainly the easiest winders to manipulate and they are recognised as being extremely efficient. The line can be unwound, length by length, by a simple rotating movement of the wrist. This device is ideal as it offers the operator maximum freedom of movement. A well-designed winder must not have any sharp corners which could cut the line. As well as the winding surface, the winder should incorporate a cut-out handle to enable the operator to grasp the winder firmly.

The minimum thickness should be between 10 and 12 mm. If the board is any thinner, it may break. Nylon lines are more or less elastic and tend to be taut when rewound. When the line is unwound, this tension is released and can break the board. The same problem can occur with lines made from natural fibres, dampened by rain or by a high degree of humidity in the atmosphere. When they dry they shrink, and once wound they can break the board or cause distortion.

For a line of average length, the board measures 32 cm x 20 cm. The handle should be 12 cm long and the winding surface 24 cm x 10 cm. Above a certain length of line, a mechanical winder should be used. The largest winders should be fixed to the ground.

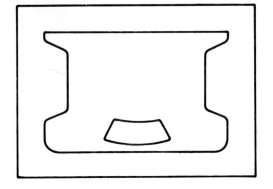

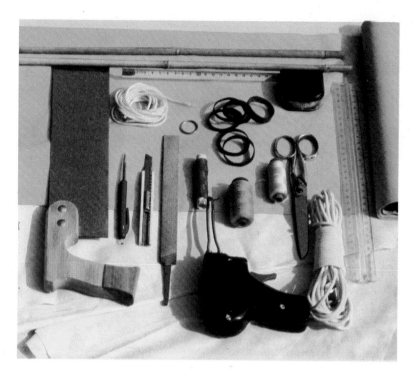

Tools and materials

Tools needed for kite-making are in the main those which are commonly used. Thus, the models described in this book can be made by everyone.

Tools and materials necessary to make a collapsible kite.

Cover	Suitable frame	Assembly	Decoration	Weight	Collapsible	Drag	Flying line
light paper	thin stick rice straw	white glue, adhesive tape	gouache, ink	very light	No	weak	sewing thread
strong paper	sorghum, cane, bamboo, rattan	glue for wood, adhesive tape, strong glue	gouache, ink, collage	light	No	weak to medium	sewing thread
silk or cotton	thin stick, rattan	glue for fabric, reinforcing tape	dyes, ink, batik	light	No	medium	linen
synthetic fabric	bamboo, deal, light alloy, polypropylene	sewing, adhesive tape	patchwork	varying from light to heavy	Yes	Medium to high	fishing line
nylon, plastic film	stick, synthetic tubing	plastic adhesive tape	marker pens, solvent	varying from light to heavy	two possibilities	high	nylon
polyethylene film	stick, synthetic tubing, light alloy fibre-glass	heat application, adhesive tape, cloth tape	marker pens, patchwork, solvent	varying from light to heavy	Yes	medium	nylon
tyvek	fibre-glass aluminium synthetic tubing	strong glue, glue for leather, synthetic resin	ink, paint, dyes	varying from light to heavy	Yes	very high	nylon
expanded polystyrene	frameless	resin, strong glue	ink, vinyl paint	light or medium	Yes	medium	nylon or natural fibre

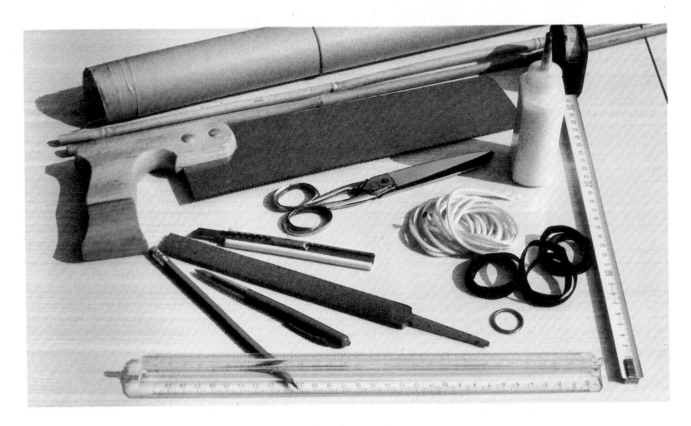

Tools and materials necessary to make a paper kite.

Paper kites

Flexible and light structures are best for paper kites. Sticks should be tested very carefully and balanced under the best conditions in order to obtain strict symmetry of dimension and weight.

Bamboo sticks have excellent qualities of strength, flexibility, lightness and durability. They are ideal for making this type of kite. After being soaked in water, they are dried by the fire and then hung with weights or heavy objects to keep them straight. When they have been soaked, they can also be bowed if desired.

Since the weight of a bamboo stick is distributed rather unevenly throughout its length, each stick should be whittled or sand-papered until it is as evenly balanced as possible. Several attempts may be necessary before you have a completely balanced frame. In some cases, you may have to fix a counterweight at the end of the cross-sticks in order to counterbalance them.

The best way of joining two cross-sticks is by lashing them together with cotton or linen thread. Be careful that the thread does not cut into the wood since this will affect the strength of the sticks and therefore create weak spots in the construction of the kite. After the sticks have been lashed together, the ends of the thread should be glued to reinforce the insulation of the join, since moisture may affect the tension of the thread.

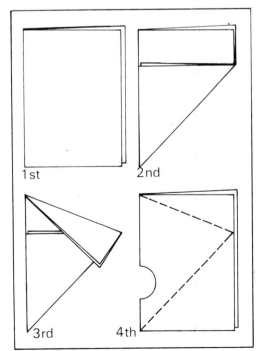

Folding the cover.

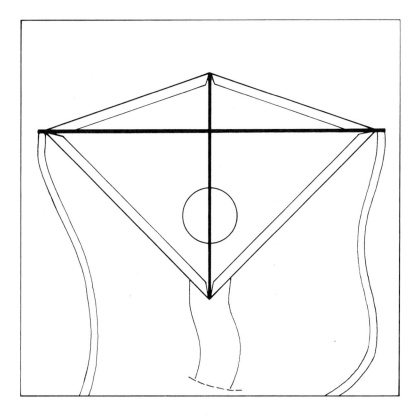

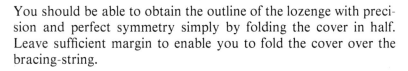

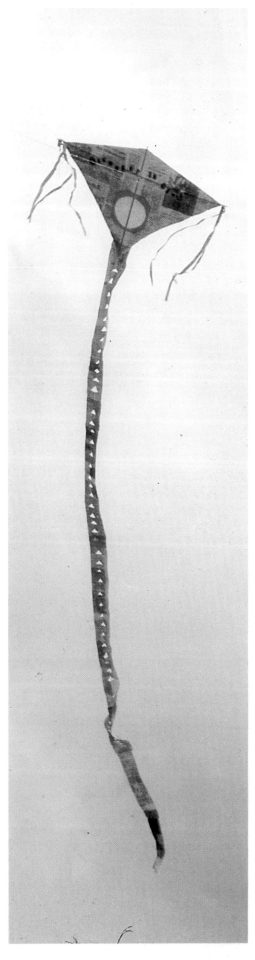

You should be able to obtain the outline of the lozenge with precision and perfect symmetry simply by folding the cover in half. Leave sufficient margin to enable you to fold the cover over the bracing-string.

Before doing this, check the measurements and symmetry of the frame and secure the bracing-string at each point. Fix the tail with a loop on the back of the spine.

The cover needs to be applied to the frame quickly. The English method, where the paper is stretched, is ideal. The paper is placed between two damp cloths and dried slowly and steadily before being put onto the frame.

If the cover is curved, cut notches into the curved edges so that they can be turned over neatly. Turn the edges of the cover over the bracing-string. Flour paste is ideal for this, particularly if it has been heated gently first.

Reinforce the bridling points with glue by slipping it between the frame and the cover.

For the tail, cut strips of coloured paper two to three centimetres wide and attach them at regular intervals onto the tail string, which should be seven times the length of the kite. If preferred, a long strip of paper and smaller strips, as for the tail, can also be attached to the ends of the cross-sticks.

Japanese kites

The types of frame for Oriental kites are as varied as the subjects depicted in their decoration. The collection presented in this book aims to show the principal types of kites in the East. The predominance of Japanese kites shows the important part they still play in the long Japanese tradition. Above all, they are witness to a mythology which is still very much alive, and the subject of a great culture. All the "takos" (Japanese for kite) are regarded as carrying "a prayer written to the spirit of the wind".

After being unpopular for a while, kite-flying in Japan has returned to public favour. Each region has adopted a particular form of construction and decoration for its kites. In Yoskosuka, for example, a falcon is the most popular symbol. In Nagoya, the main subject is a brightly-coloured insect. The "Beka" is a tiny kite which is very difficult to fly because it is made of a large number of sticks. In Sugura, kites represent Kabuki actors and warriors, and the theme of waves if often used.

The irregular pentagonal shape of the kites presented here (similar in form to a shield) has been designed by Mitsuo Okatake, of Osaka. The subjects are based on the actors of a puppet theatre (the Burunku theatre), amongst them being the monk, the trader, the famous Samurai, the cunning tiger-hunting hero, the mature woman, portrayed with closed mouth and shaved eyebrows, the young girl with half-open mouth (symbol of eroticism), the Geisha, the round-eyed robber, etc.

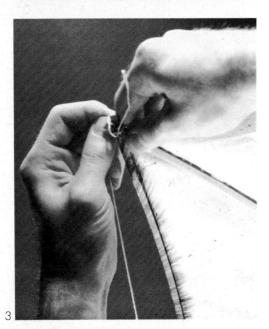

For centuries, the kite-making tradition has been passed down from father to son. Motifs and colours are inspired by old paintings. Bamboo sticks, rice paper, powder paint, string, a long-bladed knife, some glue and the wind – nothing else is needed to fly one of these marvellous "Takos". Takos are flat kites which are bowed at the front, depending on the wind. To be well-balanced, it is essential that they are perfectly symmetrical. As for the Western kites, the rule remains unchanged. In Japan, tails are seldom attached to the kites, for it would mean that the kite flew badly, and would be looked upon with contempt. On the other hand, pompons are used to absorb air moisture.

The takos of Mitsuo Okataké, a famous solitary kite-flyer, can climb up to 5000 metres. Their ascent can sometimes take more than 10 minutes, and once they have reached 1000 metres they can no longer be seen. Then Okataké, who is not talkative by nature, starts talking to them, or tells them stories, happy or sad. He feels their impulses and their fears through the flying line, thus understanding their desires better. Often, he can be seen flying forty kites at a time, with their lines held down under stones.

Japanese kites can reach huge proportions. Some can weigh up to 1000 kilograms. Okataké once built one 10 metres high and 6 metres wide. The entire cover was made of rice paper, and was

1. Pentagonal kite, upper face – 2. Lower face – 3. Bracing the kite.

Okatake's pentagonal kites. ►

1

beautifully decorated. Kite-flying combats take place every Sunday in spring on the hills of Nagasaki. To handle a kite, it is sometimes necessary to have a team of fifty handlers and a leader who gives orders. The game consists of blocking the opponent and fallen kites belong to the first person to catch them.

The Western kite, which is regarded more as a scientific object, differs from that of the Far East both in its purpose and its design.

The lighter density of these pentagonal kites gives them less stability. In strong wind, the front spar must be braced with a bracing-string which is wound around the ends extending from the frame. The front cross-bar should be approximately equal to 3/5 the length of the longeron and the diagonal sticks equal in length to the longeron. They should cross at a point 2/5 of their length and 3/10 of the length of the longeron. They are lashed together.

The hexagonal kite was designed by Hiroï. Its frame is made of three elements: a longeron and two spars. The length of the spars is 6/9 of the length of the longeron; they are parallel and the distance between them is equal to about half of the length of the longeron. They are bowed by a string braced between each end.

The frame of the rectangular kites is generally constructed from two diagonals. The cross-bars are parallel and their number can vary (4, 5 or 6). In some cases, the frame is reinforced by three longerons equally parallel to each other. The front legs of the bridles are generally attached to the ends of the leading edge, and the other legs at the intersection of certain elements of the frame.

2

1. and opposite: rectangular kite (Hashimoto) – 2. and 3. Hexagonal kite – 4. Traditional Japanese kite.

3

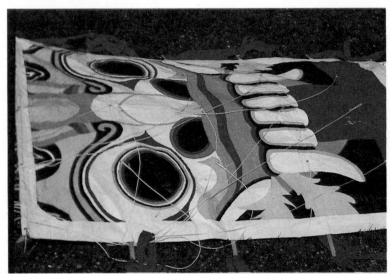

4

The Thai Serpent

The Thai Serpent is the most representative of the kites from Thailand. It is recognised by its flat cover, which is usually rounded, and has a very long tapering tail which can measure up to 6 metres.

Its frame is made of a curved stick outlining its shape and determining the surface of the cover, a 45-cm longeron and a 30-cm spar which strengthens the leading edge and prevents it from becoming distorted. Both ends of the curved sticks are braced by a bow-string. Two small tails are attached to each side.

The model illustrated is of a very light construction and has little wind resistance. It is best flown in light winds. From its construction it is immediately recognisable as a member of the flat kite group.

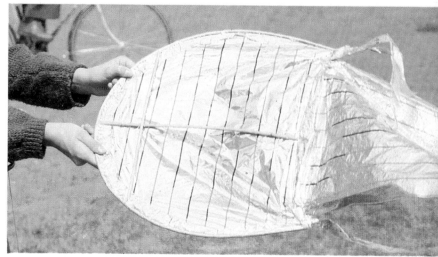

The Chinese Bird

The most complex structures can be found among traditional Chinese kites, this Chinese bird being an example.

The technique used for making these kites requires great accuracy in the measurement of the sticks, their adjustment and their assembly. The different parts are, as for the dragon-fly, entirely collapsible and fastened to each other by means of metal joints. The tail, for example, is a sort of hinged "clapper" fastened to the body of the bird in two places. The whole kite is made of four main parts: the body of the bird, its two wings and its tail.

The body is formed by a small fuselage made of two curved sticks which determine the width of the body, and a spine, also curved, on which five spars are fixed. The head is part of the body and is in fact an extension of the fuselage. Painted rice paper covers the lower face of the kite. The back of the bird is covered by a light "lid".

The wings are also made of paper, their leading edge being made rigid by a stick running along the wing. It is fastened to the back of the bird's body.

Exotic butterfly.

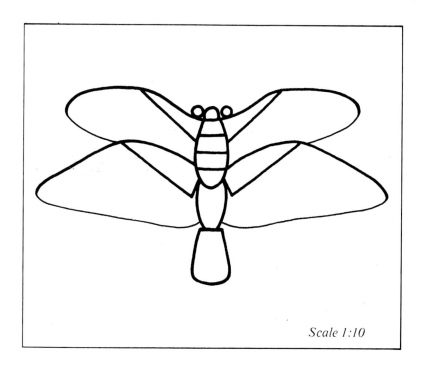

Scale 1:10

The tail is separate. It has a flat frame which is shaped by one curved stick.

This Chinese bird will present a real challenge to the careful kite designer since its design and assembly are very delicate. But he is sure to get great pride and pleasure from it!

The exotic butterfly

This is a variation of the Chinese bird, also belonging to the family of dihedral kites. The fuselage is made of only four spars and the back of the fuselage is extended to form the flat lower half of the body to which the tail is attached. There are four wings, each supported by a brace.

Decoration

The way kites are decorated is very closely linked to the type of cover and the material from which it is made. For example, it is difficult to dye material made from synthetic fibres, and even more difficult to paint it. The decorations described here are more suitable for covers made from paper or light material. Needless to say, the cover must be decorated before being applied to the frame. All sorts of techniques can be used, from the simplest to the most complicated.

Paper covers can be painted with gouache or vinyl paint, then varnished with a brush or a spray to protect them from moisture. The design can be inspired by various motifs and should be sketched onto the cover before painting. This technique will give you maximum flexibility.

Coloured paper can also be used and it should be slightly dampened before being placed on the frame.

The usual printing techniques can be used for silk and light fabrics: batik (soaking the fabric in ink-based dyes), etc. Permanent inks should be used.

Large pieces of woven cloth provide many ideas for decoration. As they often include many designs, they can thus be used to make covers.

Paint or ink cannot be applied to plastic film, for they cannot be fixed and the colours would inevitably fade. Instead, solvents and special varnishes are used. You can also use marking pens which retain the brilliance of the colours and do not impair the transparency of the film.

The decoration of covers in synthetic fabric tends to be rather restricted. Different coloured pieces can be sewn together. To do this, prepare a pattern beforehand with the exact position of the pieces making up the design. As a large variety of fabrics are available, kite-flyers should be able to match colours without much difficulty. It is best to avoid double thickness, as well as pockets, which would only make the kite needlessly heavier.

Kites in expanded polystyrene should be decorated with synthetic paints. Since they are rigid and the paint can be fixed, they are ideally suited for decoration. But be careful not to give too thick a coat of paint which would make the kite heavier. For clear and precise designs, surround the areas to be painted with adhesive film.

Some kite-flyers decorate their kites very simply with marking pens.

1. and 2. Different stages in the decoration of a paper kite, using ink –
3. Paper kite painted – 4. and 5. Light paper kites.

Construction of a collapsible kite

The collapsible square is a flat kite with a tail. As it is easy to make, it is very suitable for beginners. It can fly in both moderate and strong winds (approximately 4 metres per second). A flying line with a break strength of 60 kg should be used, but don't forget to wear protective gloves.

We suggest making the cover out of non-porous fabric – nylon, terylene, spinnaker (very thick nylon). But you can adapt our instructions and use cheaper material if you wish (kraft paper, for instance). In this case, the seams will have to be glued instead of sewn.

For an 80-cm square, buy a square metre of fabric. The extra material will be used to make the bows of the tail.

Making up the kite

a) Fold the nylon in two so that the corners meet exactly. Allow 1.5 cm along each edge of the square for the seams.

b) Cut the nylon, using a soldering-iron rather than a pair of scissors or a cutter. By melting the nylon whilst it is being cut, it should prevent the material from unravelling. Protect your work table from the heat of the soldering-iron.

c) Fold the edge of the nylon in by 5 mm and press it with a warm iron (make sure that it is on "synthetic"). Fold a second time and press. This will save you having to pin the fabric and make it easy to hem by machine.

d) Hem the four sides of the square to reinforce them. Although, since the invention of sophisticated sewing machines, sewing is no longer the prerogative of women, men will sometimes, let's admit it, need a woman's advice.

e) Draw the diagonals of the square in order to find the centre. Place a penny in the centre and cut around it to make a hole. The edges of the hole should be reinforced with a second small piece

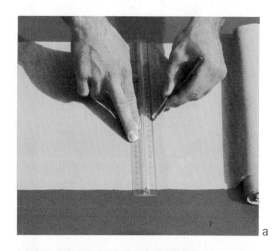

a

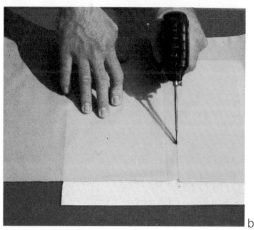

b

c

c

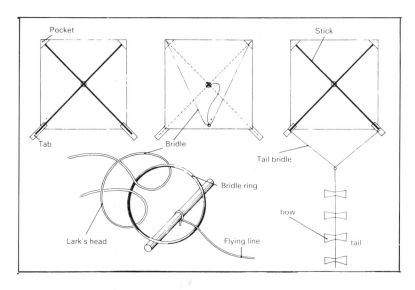

Pocket   Stick

Tab   Bridle

Tail bridle

Bridle ring

Lark's head   Flying line

bow

tail

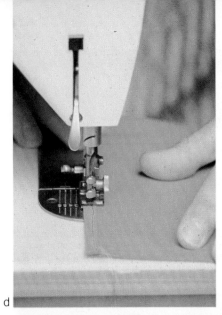

e

f

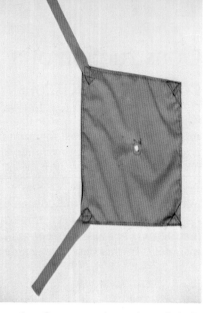

d

g

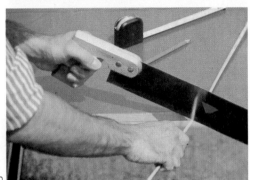

h

i

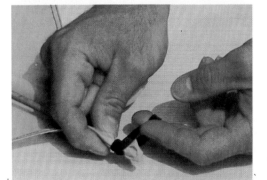

j

k

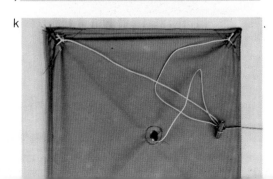

of nylon. This is to prevent the nylon from wearing where it is in contact with one of the bridle legs which will be added later.

f) Make two pockets by cutting two 10-cm squares with the soldering iron. Fold them diagonally and sew them into the two corners of the main square. The two sticks will be fitted into these pockets.

g) Still using the soldering-iron, cut two tabs 5 x 20 cm. Sew them onto the other two corners following the line of the diagonals. These tabs will be folded over the other two ends of the sticks and fastened.

The cover is now complete and the frame should be assembled.

h) Take a bamboo stick 1 cm in diameter and saw it into two sticks 16 cm long. Using a wood file or some sandpaper, smooth the ends in order to prevent the cover from being torn.

i) Insert each stick into its pocket.

j) Fold the two tabs over both sticks, making sure that the cover is taut. Fasten them using thread or a rubber band (perhaps cut from an old inner tube of a bike).

k) The bridle is a two-legged bridle:
— one leg is 1.8 m long, tied to the ends of the bamboo sticks in their respective pockets. You will have to pierce two holes in each pocket with the soldering-iron, one each side of the stick.

— the second leg is 50 cm long, lashed to the middle of the first leg and to the intersection of the two sticks, thus joining them together.

Next, fasten the bridle ring to the towing point with a lark's head knot. The flying line is attached to this ring.

The bridle of the tail is made of a leg 1.6 m long. Fasten each end to the tabs of the cover using a slip knot, then fasten a ring to the middle of the bridle. The tail will be attached to this ring.

The length of the tail is ten times the length of the square. Using the remaining material, cut out bows 5 x 15 cm and tie them to the tail every 20 cm.

The regular hexagonal

The regular hexagonal is a flat kite which needs a tail to fly.

The cover is relatively simple to make. Choose four colours – red, blue, yellow and light blue, for example – in synthetic material.

Cut the red and blue pieces methodically, using the first one as a template for the next five. The yellow circles are cut in the same way. The blue circle will be made later. The red and blue pieces should be sewn together with a double seam by machine and the outer edges hemmed. The circular windows are cut out using a semicircular template: fold the fabric half, place the template along the fold and cut around the semicircle. Afterwards, the yellow and light blue circles are sewn into place, preferably by machine.

The frame is made using three sticks of equal length which are inserted in the pockets provided at each corner of the seams. Two pockets out of six are "removable". These are small tabs which are folded over the ends of the sticks, and fastened with string.

The sticks are then lashed together in the middle of the cover to hold them in position.

Regular hexagonal.

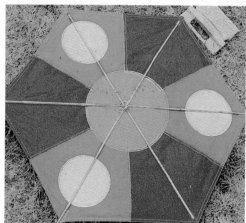

Central joint of the star.

The star kite, five-point

This is a variation of the regular pentagonal. Its frame is made by using five sticks of equal length, held in position centrally by a plastic joint. A fastening point for the rear leg is attached to one of the sticks 3/5 of the way along its length. Three of the sticks are placed on one side of the cover, whilst the remaining two are placed on the opposite side.

The same system of assembly is used for the points of the star as for the regular hexagonal. In our model, the cover is made from fabric in three colours: orange, yellow and green for the border. The different pieces are sewn together by machine.

The Centipede

Scale 1:16

This very old kite, the centipede, has always been known in China. This is a flat kite made of a large number of discs of decreasing diameter, attached by two lateral strings. Each disc is made from paper or from plastic film. They are made rigid by using bamboo sticks which extend on each side of the disc by a length equal to twice the diameter. Little stabilising ribbons are attached to each end of the bamboo sticks.

The disc with the largest diameter (60 cm) is used to make the head, whilst the rest of the discs decrease from 50 to 39 cm. Each is spaced from the next by a distance equal to their radius.

The model shown is made from tyvek using the silk screen process (with printing inks).

The centipede is particularly suitable for moderate and steady winds.

The Carp

This marvellous carp is one of the fabulous traditional Japanese fish kites, whose construction is based on the principle of the windsock. The air blows through the windsock and the air flow is regulated automatically. As for all windsocks, the frame is very basic. Only three cross-sticks are used, equal to the width of the fabric, attached laterally to the two parallel longerons. The bridle is attached in two places to a separate lower longeron.

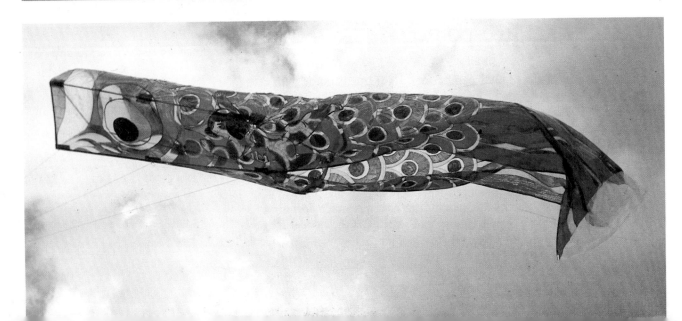

The Giant Bird

The wing span of this gentle bird, a member of the flat kite family, is not less than three metres. With its very flexible structure and its apparently vulnerable shape, this kite needs to be carefully and precisely assembled. The diagram below shows the main elements of the frame, the tying points, and the position of the guys.

The frame is made from eight very flexible bamboo sticks. The two largest, inserted in the sleeves provided, form the leading edge of the wing. The four sticks used for the tail are attached to the spine in two places, and their opposite ends are joined together to form an inverted 'V' shape.

As you may imagine, this kite is a good flier in light and moderate winds, but avoid flying it in strong winds.

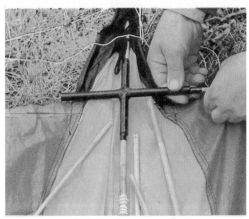

Inserting the bamboo sticks in the joint. Method of attaching the elements of the frame to the spine.

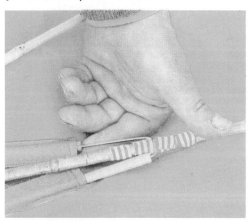

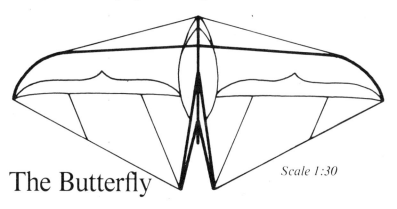

The Butterfly

Scale 1:30

Here is a kite remarkable for its balanced proportions. Its wings are perfectly symmetrical and form a dihedral angle. They are concentric and are made from fabric beautifully sewn together.

Its frame is very simple. Two sticks, which are slightly curved for the upper section, are crossed and inserted in their respective sleeves, provided in the cover.

The lower ends of the sticks are attached using the classical method (tabs), which is found in the square kite and in many others.

The body of the butterfly is made with a second frame, made rigid by longerons.

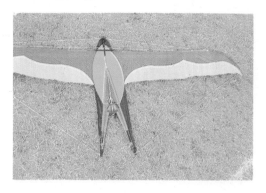

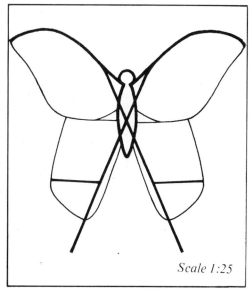

Scale 1:25

The Dragon, the Cobra, and the Butterfly

A single frame but three different models, such are the advantages of this kite with its adaptable structure taken from the dihedral kite.

The frame, made from Dural, is the same for each of the three models. It consists of:

— a short longeron with two braces at its tail end which are used to join the two rear sticks of the pentagonal cover.

— a front spar made of two sticks and joined to the longeron.

— a small mast to hold the elements of the frame tight and in position.

— a horizontal brace joining both sticks of the spar together.

The tension is adjusted by sliding the braces along the longeron.

The shape of the cover is similar to the Eddy. However, a tail 26 m long and 80 cm wide is attached to the base of the kite. This tail, in fact, gives the cover its fifth side.

The cover of these three kites is made from polyethylene, but other materials such as Dacron or rayon can also be used.

1. Butterfly – 2. – 4. Cobra – 3. Adjustment of the cover – 5. Dragon.

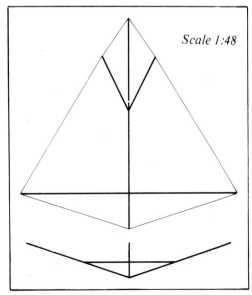

Scale 1:48

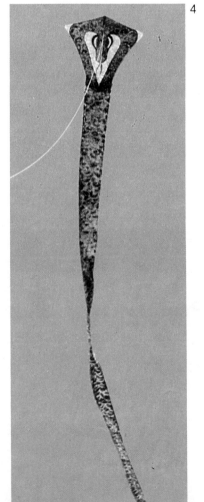

The Eddy

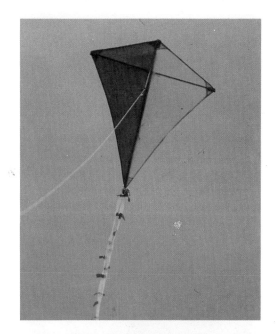

The Eddy is undoubtedly the best example of a dihedral kite. Its flat cover forms a perfect, finely proportioned dihedral angle along the spine.

As for many kites, it can be built on different scales as it is a good flier. The only possible drawback may be the strength of its components. For larger dimensions, a strong frame as well as the approiriate flying line must be used. The Eddy has also been built on a very small scale, the smallest model being no more than 20 cm long.

Although this kite is very easy to make, a little skill is needed to cut the fabric and assemble the sticks.

The frame of the Eddy kite is made from two sticks of equal length, thus differing from the frame of the Diamond kite which is so popular in North America. The Eddy flies very differently – it is based on the geometry of the Malay kites, and can fly without a tail.

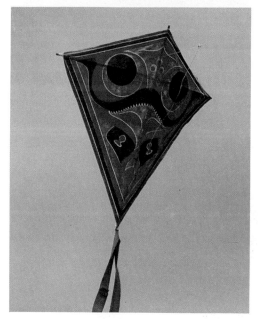

In general, the elements of the frame should cross 4/5 or 3/4 of the way along the longeron, from the tail end.

The bridling points should also be situated 1/6 and 2/3 of the way along the length of the longeron, still measuring from the tail end.

Once the cover is stretched taut, certain distortions may appear. This is why it is best to make the cover out of fabric.

To make assembly easier, hem the edges of both wings over the framing line.

Make small notches at each end of the sticks to secure the frame lines.

Finally, adjust the cover onto the frame and attach the bridle – your kite is now ready for its first trial flight.

As the spar is subject to a certain amount of tension it is wise to reinforce the centre of the framework by attaching a smaller stick to the spar (it should be about 1/3 of the length of the spar).

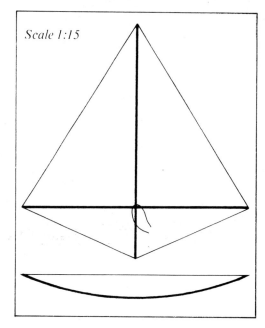

Scale 1:15

Double-sailed roller

This is a large light kite which belongs to the group of bowed or dihedral kites. It is best flown in light winds of low velocity, for its light flexible structure is unsuited to the turbulence of strong winds.

Strong material, such as nylon, should be used for the cover. If the cover is made of several sections they should be sewn together, as in the case of the hexagonal or star kites. To obtain perfect symmetry, the main surface should be folded in half lengthwise, and both thicknesses of cloth cut together. In fact, most of the covers are cut using this technique. The cover is then unfolded, and cut according to the design.

The cover is made in two separate sections, linked together by two fasteners 15 cm long.

The frame follows a classical design, made from a longeron 150 cm long and two spars 120 cm long.

The essential characteristic of this kite is that it has two small masts, attached to the intersection of the spars with the longeron. The tips of these small masts are notched and secure the guys holding the spars and the longeron to prevent any distortion. The masts are designed to be attached to the longeron, as shown in Fig. 1. Each guy has a sliding guy adjustor to adjust its height.

With the exception of the front spar, the parts of the frame are placed in sleeves provided in the seams.

The guys are attached to the ends of the spars and longeron with a toggle and ring (Fig. 2). The ring is fastened with a piece of cord at the corner of the cover. The cover is attached to the frame, using tabs folded over the spar and held in position with rubber bands. The roller also has a small keel, a rudder and a three-legged bridle. One of the legs is fastened to the keel, the other to the rudder.

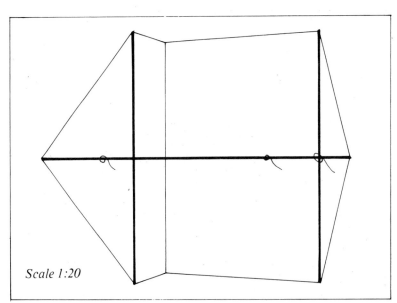

1. Separate mast – 2. Fastening the cover to the ends of the spars – 3. Rudder – 4. Lower face of the kite.

Scale 1:20

The W Form Kite

The W Form kite is classed as a cellular kite, although its cover is not made of real closed cells.

The four sections of the frame give the kite its characteristic W shape, which is made in two parts. The six longerons are arranged on two levels, four on the upper and two on the lower, and thus form the W shape.

The kite is made rigid by two long spars which extend by about 25 cm on each side of the kite. Guys are attached using rings and made taut.

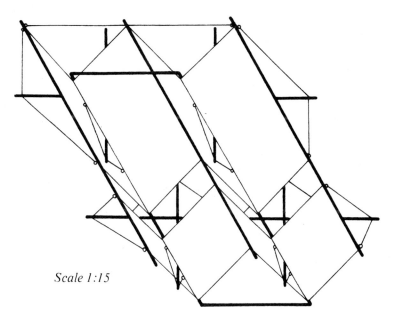

Scale 1:15

The W Form kite is perfect for flying in moderate winds.

The Triple Conyne Kite

As all the types of Conyne kites, the triple Conyne is a flexible cellular kite. The upper four longerons are made rigid by only one spar.

The cover is made in several sections. The main surface, made from materials using natural or synthetic fibres, is fixed to the upper longerons. Each cell is made from two pieces of cloth which form a small dihedral angle opening on to the main surface of the cover and attached to the upper longerons. The lower independent longerons form the point of each cell, and the six bridling points are attached to them, two per longeron.

The triple conyne flies very well in light to moderate winds.

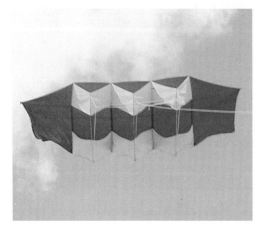

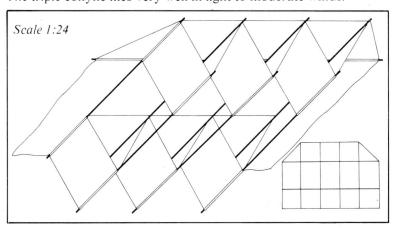

Scale 1:24

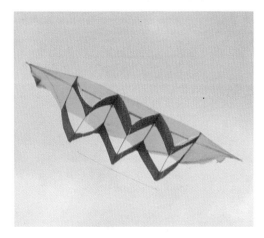

The Plano

The plano is also a flexible cellular kite. It is made of two classical V-shaped cells (as those of the triple conyne) attached to the two longerons of the upper section of the frame. The point of the V of both cells is formed by a third lower longeron.

Here again, the main part of the cover is made rigid by a long spar. The small spar ensures that the distance between the two longerons remains perfectly parallel.

The total span is 1.95 m. This measurement is in fact equal to the length of the two sticks forming the spar and is the longest in the plano.

The longerons are one metre long and are made preferably from poplar, whilst walnut is used for the two small cross sticks. The cross stick of the rear section is inserted in a sleeve.

The cover is made from several segments radiating from a large circle. Synthetic fabric is used and all the pieces are sewn together.

The cover is fastened to the frame in the standard way. Each end of the main spar is fastened with tabs.

The plano has a four-legged bridle, tied to each cell and to both ends of the spar.

The plano has all the characteristics of an excellent flyer, and is particularly suitable for light or moderate winds.

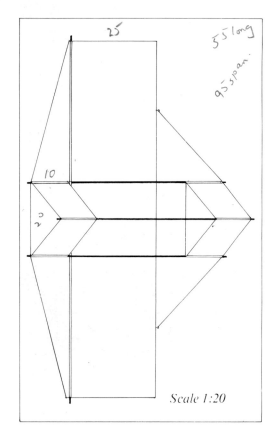

25

55 long

95 span

10

2
2

Scale 1:20

The simple three-celled kite

The frame of the three-celled kite is a large square based parallelpiped formed by four wooden longerons. These are held rigid by diagonal struts through the cells.

There are four triangular wings, each being separate and attached to one of the two spars. The rear spar is approximately one-third shorter than the front spar. They are both positioned in the same diagonal plane.

This particular model has three 45-cm cells, set at a distance of 32 m. Some models only have two.

Initially, the square-celled kites were designed more often than not without wings and with only two cells. Walter Brook, the kite-maker, designed many variations with different sorts of triangular wings.

The bridling is standard. It is a simple two-legged bridle, fixed to the front and rear of the kite.

Variant with fin

This recent variant is constructed in transparent plastic film. The cover is modified in two places. Firstly, the two large front wings are moved up and attached to the uppermost section of the kite. Secondly, a third rear wing (fin) is added, perpendicularly to the other two rear wings.

This variant differs from the simple three-celled kite, in that it has a number of guys joining the rear wings together and joining the large wings to the main body.

The three-celled kite has a four-legged bridle.

The three-celled kites fly easily in moderate winds as their structure is very strong.

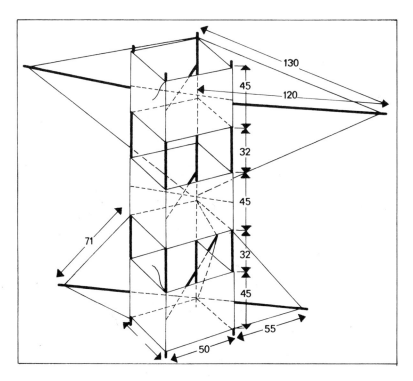

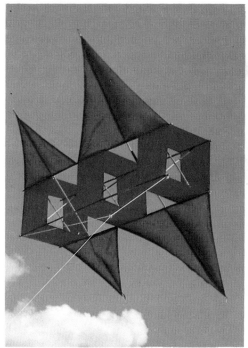

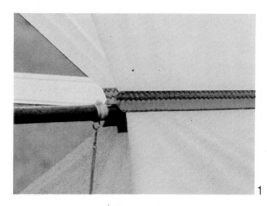

The Star

The geometry of this kite is very special. Its shape comes from three large overlapping squares which meet on their diagonal.

The frame is made from fibreglass connected in the centre by a plastic joint. The cover is cut in twelve identical trapezoidal shapes, the longest side forming the edge of the square.

The centre of the kite is thus left open, which enables the airflow to be better distributed throughout the kite.

The cover is made from spinnaker.

The kite can be larger or smaller than the model pictured, as long as the relationship between the proportions and the principle of density is respected.

The star-shaped kite is a good flyer in strong wind, and also performs quite well in moderate wind.

The cover is fastened at the end of each element of the frame with tabs.

1. Attaching the legs of the bridle – 2. and 3. Attaching the cover to the ends of the spars using Velcro tape – 4. Central joint.

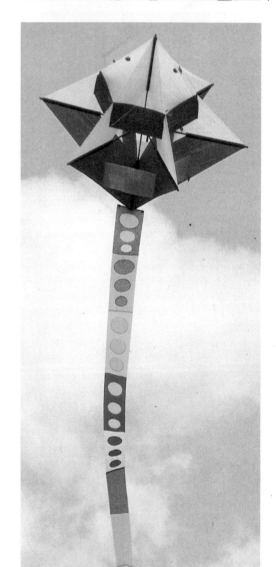

The Cody

This kite has a long history. On many occasions it enabled Cody to carry out "human ascents". He designed a train technique flying six kites on a single flying cable wound on a mechanical winch. It is also with this very kite that Cody flew across the Channel in 1903.

The Cody is a box-kite with two large wings and six small wings, along with two cells, divided in the centre.

The kite is of average density, and flies well in both moderate and stronger winds. It can be built to a larger or smaller scale, the largest models reaching a wing span of 4.50 m. The model shown has a wingspan of 1.80 m, corresponding to the original scale, which is the ideal size.

The material used for the cover should be carefully chosen and be particularly suited to this type of kite. Cotton or linen fabric is generally used to ensure that in flight the cover retains its shape and the appropriate tension. The edges of the cover are consequently slightly concave between the elements of the frame. This particular shape, which earned the nickname of "The Bat", enables the tension to be better distributed.

The rigidity comes from the design of the frame. The elements of the frame cross in the centre of the cells, thus giving uniformity to the whole kite.

They project from the cover, and adjustments can be made from all eight projecting points.

The Saconney

The Saconney, after the name of its designer, is very similar to the Cody. It was used for experiments in 1909. The French army adopted it for its system of fastening kites flying in train and used it during the First World War.

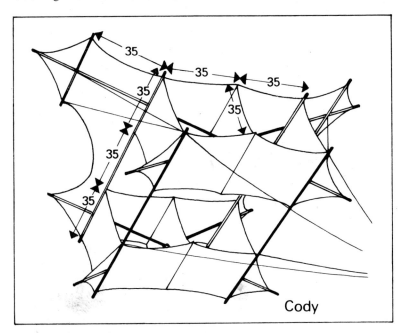

Cody

1. and 3. Cody – 2. Saconney.

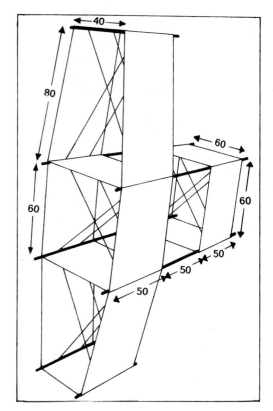

The Pomoserf

Based on Hargrave's kites, the Pomoserf is a box-kite designed to fly in rather strong wind. Because of its solid structure, the main characteristics of the pomoserf are its robustness and its compactness. It is in fact the forerunner of the biplane. The shape of its frame suggests the first aeroplanes.

The frame is made rigid by struts which form the divisions within the cells.

The cover is placed around the frame. The two vertical walls of the central cell are aligned to those of the tail.

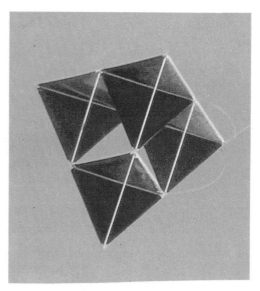

The Bell

This kite belongs to the large family of tetrahedral kites developed between 1902 and 1904 by Alexander Graham Bell. The model shown is made of four tetrahedral cells, the length of the edge being 25 cm.

The ideal material for the frame is thermoplastic tubing. It gives strength to the kite, particularly in the case of multi-celled kites. The ends of the elements of the frame can be worked under heat without difficulty. Where parts need to be glued together, a synthetic resin should be used.

The cover is made from plastic. Sleeves are provided for the frame. Hems are not necessary.

Bell kites fly well without a tail, and are good fliers in moderate or strong wind. In most cases they are not collapsible.

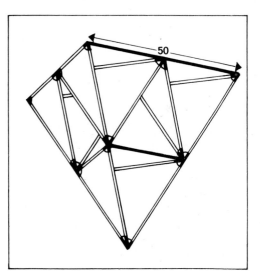

The Umbrella

As its name suggests, this kite is based on the same principle as the umbrella, although it is an improved design as it can be folded into two sections. It is easy to carry. The cover, divided into segments, forms a large regular octagonal. It is made of a central section, a peripheral section, and vents, and attached to a star-shaped bamboo frame. The whole kite is held rigid with guys.

In strong wind the surface of the cover can be reduced by folding over the peripheral element of the frame. The umbrella is best flown in moderate winds.

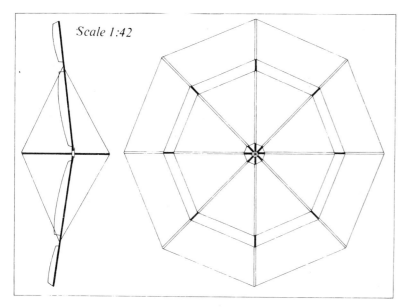

Scale 1:42

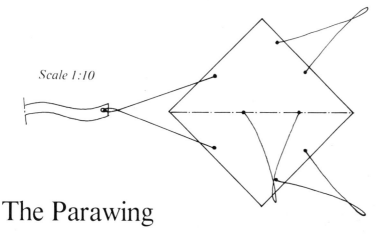

Scale 1:10

The Parawing

Like parafoils, parawings do not have a solid frame. They are made using a simple square of cloth or plastic (taken from a large plastic bag, for instance, as used for the model shown).

The parawing has a compound bridle, made of six legs (i.e. three strings joined to the towing point). The outer legs are attached to the two leading edges, forming the nose of the kite. The two other legs are positioned along the diagonal axis of symmetry of the cover.

Because of its frameless design, the parawing is well suited to light winds. It is not very stable, so a ribbon 70 cm long can be attached to form a tail.

1

2

3

4

5

1. Central joint – 2. The hinged section of the frame – 3. Lower face of the kite – 4. Side view – 5. Parawing.

49

The Flexifoil

Like the stunter, the flexifoil is a dirigible kite.

It is made of small units of synthetic fabric, similar in shape to a simple bag, and joined to both flying lines with a cross bar. This kite is very easy to handle, and can perform many acrobatic movements in flight.

Each unit is rectangular and sewn on three sides. A strip of very loosely woven fabric is sewn to the leading edge (fourth side) so that the wind can inflate the cover when taking off. These kites differ from the parafoils in that they do not have cells. The cover is made rigid by a cross-bar running along the leading edge. It is fastened to the two flying lines by a lark's head knot, secured by two small toggles.

In flight, it is vital to take into account the number of units of the cover. If there are too many, there will be too much drag on the flying lines in a strong wind. It will be difficult to handle the kite, and the handler may even be lifted from the ground. Obviously, moderate winds are to be preferred!

The two flying lines are attached to each end of the cross-bar winding reel to facilitate handling.

1. Flexifoil with 9 units – 2. Controlling the flexifoil using a cross-bar winder – 3. Method of attaching the units – 4. Flexifoil with 3 units.

The Stunter

The stunter is designed to offer maximum manoeuvrability. It belongs to the group of dirigible kites, i.e. it has a double flying line connected to two separate reels held – one in each hand – by the handler; thus, the stunter really can be manoeuvred. By pulling on the line, it can perform various acrobatic movements (large circles, loops, zig zags, etc.).

The construction of the stunter is not very difficult. Its frame is similar to the delta kite. However, the spine is much longer and the wings form a perfect right angle.

A special bridling system is used, made of two bridles with three legs each. The first leg is fastened to the tail end of the spine, the second to the cover, and the third to the leading edge.

The Delta Kite

The delta is certainly the most well known of the kites with a keel. Its name comes from its triangular shape which is similar to the Greek letter "delta". Apart from a few improvements such as its "movable" nose, the kite has not been greatly modified since it was first designed.

The three main elements of the frame are nearly all the same length. They include a spine and two sticks running along the edges of the isosceles triangle which is formed by the cover. The whole kite is made rigid by a spar which is situated 4/7 of the way along the spine (from the tail end of the kite). The cover can be made out of synthetic material.

The keel is a triangle, the base of which is situated under the spine, its three angles being 60°, 30°, and 90° at the bridling point.

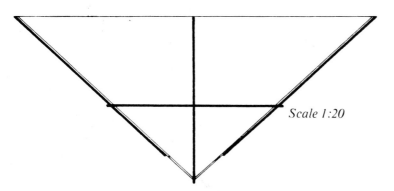

Scale 1:20

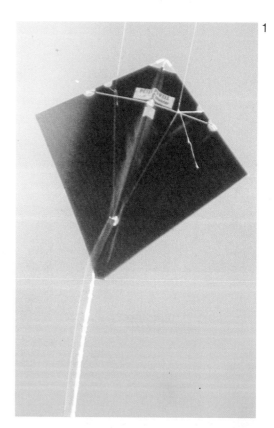

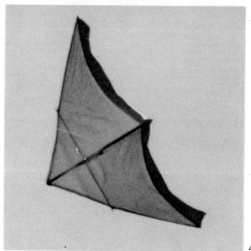

1. Lower face of stunter –
2. Stunters flying in train –
3. Winding reel of stunter –
4. Delta kite.

The Sled

Like the parawings, the frame of the sled has no spar to make it rigid, as in cellular and flat kites. Several models have been designed with vents of various shapes or even without vents (although this last type is not recommended in a strong wind because the kite would be unbalanced; this would result in the kite looping and losing altitude).

The sled flies best in light and steady winds, when it can climb easily. It is one of the rare kites which can fly with an angle of flight which varies between 50° and 60°.

Only two longerons form its frame (although in certain models there may be three). These longerons are parallel and the distance between them is equal to half their length. In most models, they are sewn into the cover.

The surface of the cover is an irregular hexagonal and the longerons form a large rectangle.

The vents can be circular, trapezoidal or simply triangular.

The material used is generally synthetic fabric or plastic film, cut in one piece with a very sharp knife. The sides of the cover are triangular and form the towing points of the legs of the bridle. They do not need hemming.

In general, the sled flies very well without a tail, although you may have to add a tail in strong wind.

As is the case with many kites, the adjustment of the bridle is the essential factor of stability and must be very carefully done.

1. Fastening the legs of the bridle –
2. Lower face of the sled –
3. Unfolded.

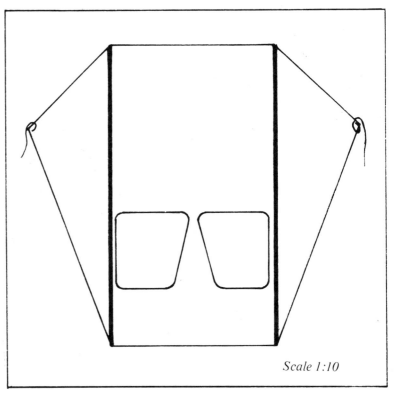

Scale 1:10

The Parafoil

The Parafoil has no frame and is made of a multi-cellular cover (like a huge bag) and a complex multi-legged bridling system fastened at the top of the ventral fins.

There are several sorts of parafoils, all based on the principle of the multi-cellular cover.

There can be from four to twelve small cells made from fabric. They are formed by two large rectangular pieces of cloth, joined at one end and open at the other, and by smaller pieces of cloth forming the walls of the cells and sewn perpendicularly between the two main rectangles. The leading edge is open, and the kite is inflated by the wind in flight, which enables it to retain its shape.

Lateral stability is obtained by attaching ventral fins along the walls of the cells underneath the cover. There are four per wall.

The simplest bridling system consists of running a leg from the top of one ventral fin to the next, passing through the bridle ring. All the legs of the bridle are mounted in this way.

Large parafoils are good flyers in moderate winds. Two people are needed for the take-off. While the first person lifts the towing point, the second holds the cover by the leading edge so that the wind inflates the cells.

A pocket balance can be used to measure the amount of tension exerted on the flying line. This little device is attached to the flying line using two rings.

Some parafoils can support the weight of a man and are used as parachutes. Needless to say, these parafoils have no flying lines. Their advantage over parachutes is their manoeuvrability, their orientation ability and their directional control.

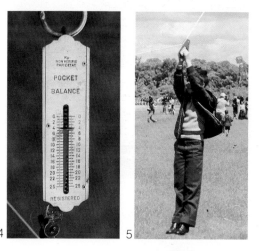

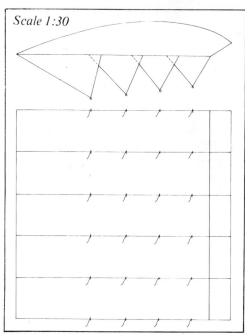

1. 10-celled parafoil – 2. 4-celled parafoil – 3. Parafoil lifting a man – 4. Pocket balance to measure the tension exerted on the flying line – 5. Young boy lifted by the drag of the parafoil

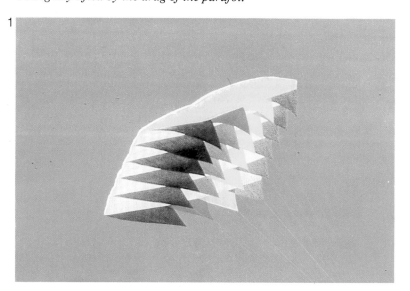

Scale 1:30

53

Kites in expanded polystyrene

Polystyrene is easy to work. The sheets can be cut with a soldering iron. They are then glued together with synthetic resin. The use of polystyrene allows greater originality of design.

Kites in polystyrene have no frame. They are relatively fragile and are not collapsible.

The Glider

The glider is made out of four sheets 1 cm thick. The upper trapezoidal sheet is joined to the square sheet of the lower section by two other strips of polystyrene which are both equal and which form the vertical walls of this single cell.

The Ball

The ball is made from four circles which are interlinked. It is assembled by cutting two of the circles so that the points of intersection form the corners of the squares. A small central keel can be added.

The Iron

This kite, very original and full of poetry, is easy to make. Its functional capacity may be subject to doubt, but it flies remarkably well.

1

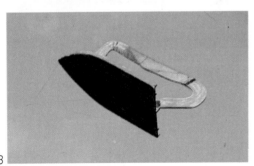

2

3

4

5

6

1. Lower face of the glider –
2. Upper face of the glider –
3. & 4. Iron –
5. 6. Ball.

The Fourré 43

This series of kites is a variation of the Diamond Kite. We can recognise the original lozenge shape of the cover, and the principle according to which the frame is built (spar and longeron). However, the spar is slightly longer and thus can carry (either lengthwise or perpendicularly) different types of helices. The spar is collapsible and can be folded along the longeron. Two small helices can be attached using a cross-bar at the tail end of the longeron.

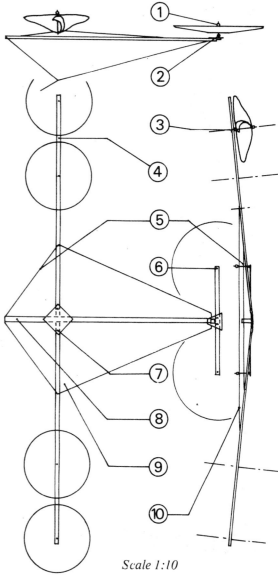

Scale 1:10

1. Small encased PVC ball.
2. PVC ball glued.
3. Piano wire 12/10 folded and glued to poplar.
4. Wing in poplar 6 x 10.
5. Piano wire 6/10 glued to cover.
6. Tail end stabiliser in poplar 2,5 x 10.
7. Pin 15/10.
8. Fuselage in poplar 8 x 8.
9. Nylon or material.
10. Adjustor in nylon thread.